THE TRAVELS OF
A CHEETAH

The Dancing Feline

Balboa Press books may be ordered through booksellers or by contacting:

Balboa Press
A Division of Hay House
1663 Liberty Drive
Bloomington, IN 47403
www.balboapress.com
1 (877) 407-4847

ISBN: 978-1-9822-0213-2 (sc)
ISBN: 978-1-9822-0214-9 (e)

Library of Congress Control Number: 2018906233

Print information available on the last page.

Balboa Press rev. date: 09/04/2019

BALBOA
PRESS
A DIVISION OF HAY HOUSE

ACKNOWLEDGEMENT

To Evelyn White, Transforming life coach and motivational speaker, after hearing about my travel experiences said, "I see a book!"

To Terence J. P. Daley, loyal friend and confidant, always supportive and always had my back.

To My Son Kevin Anthony Rout-Mayo and all of my grandchildren, my inspiration to document my legacy.

To Nancy Gallardo, professional photographer, thank you for capturing some of my magical moments on stage dancing.

To Joan Ferry Scott, for your diligence and help in bringing this book to a finish. I am most grateful.

To Christopher Anderson, for the many inspirational times as my dance instructor, confidant and friend.

INTRODUCTION

Ben and I were at LAX, ready to get our tickets and board the plane for Hong Kong, when we were told our tickets had been cancelled by Michael, our Japanese-American agent. After dealing with our initial anger and disappointment, we contacted Michael in Japan and asked why he cancelled our tickets. Surely, he would admit his error, and re-issue the tickets so we could be on our way.

*African Dance
Costume*

Michael stated that our threesome had become two and there was no communication from him before we arrived at the airport, or even when we were training. I was rude and livid. A year of preparation -- training in singing and dancing with arranged music, costing thousands of dollars, and practice, practice, practice, may all have come to naught. Well, I wasn't about to let him ruin our dream.

Michael asked to speak with the tour ticket agent. The ticket agent listened for a while, then hung up and told us to come get our tickets. We were so blessed, relieved, and ready to board, eager to begin the journey that awaited us. We loved what we trained for: dancing, singing, and choreography, and we were talented. Ben and I worked at exclusive hotels, which included room and board, and we earned fairly strong salaries. Some clubs were small and not very nice, nor large enough for real professional dancing, so we condensed our moves and altered our arranged music. Now that was fun, because even though the musicians read the notes, their music left much to be desired. In this case, whatever music they knew and expressed well, we told them to use it, and we quickly forgot about using the sheet music. Ben and I improvised on what we knew.

Our performances were strong, professional, and delighted audiences. This worked!

Preparing for performance in Malaysia

As international entertainers, we had to have working visas. By the time I returned to the States, I had accumulated seven passports with which to travel and work for my partner Ben and myself. It was an adventure that had been planned out to the last detail. But, plans can change. In the blink of an eye, plans were modified, whether or not we were ready for them. We were Americans and professionals in our field, so we worked together to keep afloat, be successful, and persevere.

Michael, the Japanese-American agent, had also cancelled all the booked shows when he cancelled our tickets. Once we arrived in Malaysia, the helpful agent, George, told us he had accomplished all he could to book us. Kuala Lumpur, Malaysia was the last booking he was able to secure for us. We thanked him and started praying. Our original contract was for eight weeks. We were out of our country, so we really were praying. At one of our performances, I met a wonderful gentleman named Terence Daley. When Terence heard of our situation, he welcomed us to stay with him while we were getting back on our feet. Thus began a second new life for me. We became good friends and lovers.

*Still modeling
at 69*

Ben and I enjoyed the new lifestyle while living in another country. We had chauffeurs en masse, servants, and the freedom to travel to other countries. I learned about life in Malaysia, as well as the Malay people, the Chinese, and Asian Indians. Each culture offered experiences in language, food, ideas, thoughts, opinions, prejudices, and more. Ben and I performed in many hotels and clubs, and we were always treated very well. Because people were curious about Americans and our culture, they loved being with us. People loved our souls and our spirits. At the time, they were very curious and wanted to know as much as possible about us. We were natural, and people loved it. They invited us into their homes to entertain us and they were very welcoming. I also met many Europeans in Malaysia and other countrymen of South East Asia and the Orient. We became friends, and to this day, we still communicate.

Unfortunately, I was accused of working without a visa. The Malay immigration authorities seemed to enjoy harassing me, because I was an American woman who had a freedom not available to many women in some cultures. To me, the authorities were the serious problem creating the stress. I never worked without my visa. I was forced to renew my visa that day, and told I had to leave the country. I was stunned and asked why. They responded by saying I was working without a visa. I told them that is a lie. I have five passports with working visas in the house. Yet and still, I was told I had two weeks to leave the country. My friend, Terence, told me not to worry. But, I was worried, because I had done nothing wrong, nor would I ever disrespect the rules of a foreign country. The stress of being harassed by a foreign government was very harmful emotionally and resulted in feelings over which I had no control.

Belly Dancing

One month before, I, and seven expatriates, had been interviewed by the *New Straits Times*, a famous Asian newspaper. We were asked questions about what we thought of our Western dress compared to the cultural dress style of the Malay women. We complemented the beauty of the Cabaya Sarong; we talked about wearing halter tops, due to the tropical weather in which we lived and worked. There were pictures of each of the ladies – nothing to brag about. In fact, the photographs were not flattering at all, and mine was the worst – my eyes were half closed! The interview was strictly political, and ultimately, I paid the price. That's why I was told to leave Malaysia.

My friend, Terence, wrote to the new Prime Minister, asking for assistance. The Prime Minister remembered the occasion when my friend had saved a Malay man from being slaughtered by an angry and revengeful Chinese mob, which sought revenge for the cultural unrest, rioting, and the murders of many Chinese in the early 1970's. The Prime Minister was happy to help Terence and me. He wrote what is called a guarded letter, telling immigration they could not stop me from entering Malaysia. In addition, they could not deport me as long as I had not broken any laws. Indeed, that was a perfect time to have a friend in high places. A few years later when the Prime Minister died, the authorities attempted again to deport me.

Preparing the African Dance

A few dollars probably would have taken care of this whole issue. I'm thinking about a show that I enjoy, *"Everybody Loves Raymond."* I understand the comedy and the dysfunction of the show. To me, it reminds me of experiences in some countries that I have been fortunate enough to visit. I get little tidbits of these cultures that make me laugh, because of who they are, especially if the program is in English.

My partner, Ben, and I sometimes found our challenges scary, but other times, they were quite wonderful. Twice, we had to defend the salary agreed upon, to keep from being cheated. Guns were involved, and though nothing happened to us, it was still frightening. Just in case, however, we always had our suitcases packed, plane tickets ready, and taxi waiting to take us to the airport. We could always go back to K.L. Malaysia, our home away from home, unlike many other performers who were forced to get to another destination for work and couldn't stay to get their money. We shared three years together, and after the last gun issue, we decided to split up. I saw him in London later that year, teaching dance and performing in a musical. It was an amazing time to see Ben, again, and watch him entertain London audiences.

I began traveling and performing solo, which I am accustomed to, and enjoy very much. My friend, Terence, and I, were very close, and he would invest in anything I tried to accomplish. We travelled to London and Paris a few times. It was a wonderful and amazing life for me. Terence wanted to marry me, but I was too independent. We would travel for his business to other Asian countries, providing the opportunity to see and understand different people and cultures. Terence was a kind, loving, and generous man. I travelled back to Malaysia a couple of times, but our relationship had changed. We always remained close friends, and he persisted in his commitment to help me, if ever I needed it. Terence passed away in September 2013. Even though I influenced his eating habits, and he welcomed it for years, he developed kidney problems and had to go on dialysis. This memoir is in loving and heartfelt memory of my friend, Terence Joseph Peter Daley.

My travels throughout South East Asia and the Orient, was a once-in-a-lifetime gift, and a life-changing set of events. Ben and I had our ups and downs, with both great and challenging experiences. That's show business for you! Once, when we were in Indonesia, our hotel had not been finished after it was built. When it rained, there was no roof intact to keep the water from getting us wet. We laughed, when Ben said, "Child, what are these people thinking?" There were always great times in Singapore, which was predominantly Chinese, and there were few problems, once we were settled in our hotel. Singapore was a great republic in which to visit and perform. I met many performers there, some I knew from past meetings in other countries. Singapore was just a fun meeting place where people were very civil, not petty, though you definitely obeyed the laws.

My Son,
Kevin
Anthony
Rout-Mayo
Six years old
at Family
Reunion

We met a German couple, who had a Boa Constrictor. Klaus, the man, would feed it a chicken, when it was hungry. One time, he forgot to wash his hands as he rubbed his stomach, which left the chicken smell there. When Klaus took the snake out of the container, it went for his stomach and gouged into his navel. He was very lucky. Then, one day, I walked into the hallway and saw the Boa Constrictor slithering against the wall. My curiosity got the better of me. I moved slowly across the hall from it and slipped one finger under its belly. I felt as if my finger was being electrocuted from the constricting snake. I yelled and fled. Klaus hurried into the hall and put it away. I could imagine what the victim feels when the snake has its body.

My years living in Asia, was the highlight of my life, before my son's birth, of course. These experiences broadened my understanding of people, places, and cultures so dramatically, that I found it difficult to re-acclimate to my own culture, when I returned home. But, I did so, regardless.

Charlotte & Chris
The Waltz

The title of my memoir is *Your Sensual Self*. The photographs of me, on the cover, and in the book, show me from my twenties, through my seventies. There is a difference, of course, but not much. I am complimented often about how I look, and I'm grateful. But, why am I grateful? I am grateful, because I enjoy how I look at this time in my life. I believe that it's because of the life I've lived, and the countries in which I've lived while dancing, singing, teaching, and learning. I'm still learning from these cultures. They have given me plenty of opportunities for understanding the richness, variety, and depth people have, who have shared their thoughts and feelings with me, and about me.

I have discovered the woman deep within my spirit, and I am bringing it to the surface. It is a beauty that has always been waiting to be discovered, to be loved, to be enjoyed, and to be me. It seeks to be expressed and to be shown to the world – family, husbands, boyfriends, friends, children, grandchildren, people I have met, and will meet, for as long as possible. But the mind can only stay focused on one culture completely while you're in it. All too soon, I returned to the view of my own culture. The effect of what I had come to know in Asia is still deep inside and can never be extinguished.

Kevin Rout-Mayo
Graduation 2019

Find your safe place, to appreciate and be grateful for who you are, and what you have received. Women are not accustomed to telling themselves how wonderful we are, and it's shameful we have allowed the world (via the media, family, and friends) to dampen our ears to ourselves.

My dancing took me to different countries to entertain. However, the chances to understand these cultures were not part of my professional dance format. I did not comprehend the changes that would happen, especially learning from the women, whose cultures I felt were Third World. I mistakenly thought they'd have something to learn from me, but I spent years, learning from them. They taught me to see the many facets of beauty, as one would view a precious gem. It's the kind of beauty that has no makeup, no subtle or subliminal mind control, telling you that you will be beautiful, only if you wear this or that.

Preparing
for Ballet
As always

I was very familiar with the media's billon-dollar campaigns, because I was from America in the 1970's. It's what American women of all colors were inundated with. They never had the chance to take a look in the mirror and tell themselves how wonderful and beautiful they are.

I have been an entertainer most of my life. In that field, you wear makeup on stage, to be seen from a distance and to enhance your face. I know that, and have done it, and I still do when performing. I also understand that as women, we like to put a little color on our faces. It can be a choice we make, not one we're controlled to make. How does one culture, nation, or organization determine what beauty is, and how it is to be applied to the world of women? I observed ladies washing clothes at the river with sarongs on their heads, wrapped beautifully. This is just one style of beauty, and there are thousands of examples like it, demonstrating various styles of beauty, in many places.

My sister Gail and I at concert.

I have lived and worked and visited in many countries throughout the world. My experiences have provided a multi-cultural view of my own beauty. I am a woman of color, beautiful and chocolate brown. And I can't, I won't say medium-chocolate, because with the African-American woman, there are so many wonderful medium chocolates to see. I love the tones of chocolate colors. The Asian women have the same tones. The hues vary, from light to dark chocolate, and there are a variety of chocolates in these cultures, too. A great part of the world is exotic. American women tend to believe that we need to change how we look to be attractive, lovely, beautiful, and accepted. The world says you can't be unique in your own understanding of beauty

The saying, "Beauty is in the eyes of the beholder," should be the American woman's mantra. Beauty has so many facets and expressions, too many to be counted. The word, beauty, blends with the words sensual and sensuality. That word represents beauty in countless ways. God has given us our senses to enjoy the beauty all around us. Being sensual can be the most rewarding experience, whether in daily life, or in more passionate times. The term, sensuality, is greatly misunderstood. Thinking that sex must mean sensual is not true. That has become an American pastime and thought.

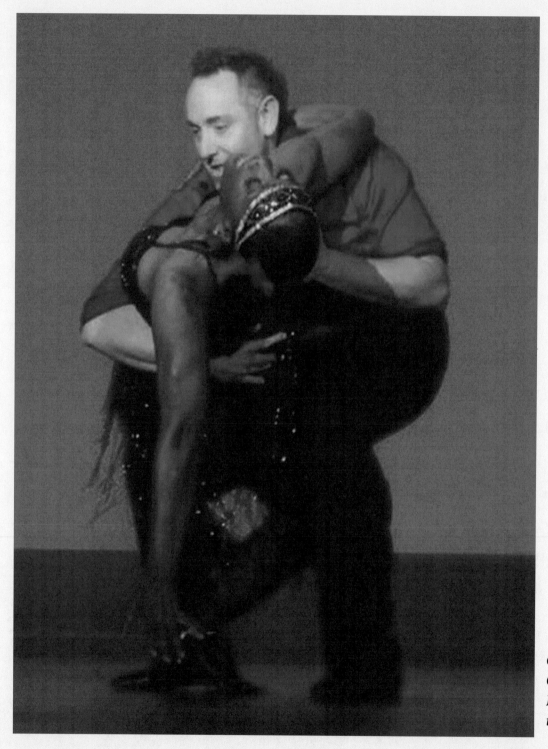

*Charlotte &
Chris 2017
Dancing with
the Stars*

Sensuality is much broader. It can be a richer ingredient for sex, but the word *sensuality* offers and expresses taste, touch, smell, hearing, and seeing. Sensual is being available for the life experiences that are waiting for us to enjoy and capture in our minds and our imagination, while being grateful for having the awareness and the ability to participate in life's gifts, everywhere. Sensuality exists in some cultures and individuals much more than others. Being sensual is simply taking the time to be aware, to feel more enriched and full of joy, which leads to harmonious life experiences. It creates a passionate spirituality and heightened awareness of yourself, others, and life itself.

The lessons learned by many young boys is, that girls and women are not to be respected, nor protected. I blame the absent fathers and stressed-out mothers, who want their daughters to be friends, and do not accept their responsibilities as mothers. These young girls grow into pre-mature women, who have not been taught to be self-respecting, nor self-loving.

We are meant to be appreciated, loved, and adored, for who we are, but our responsibility is to cherish ourselves in ways, such as: good nutrition, respect for ourselves and others by how we carry ourselves physically and verbally, and how we present ourselves to the world in our dress. These are lessons we deserve to have while growing up. We should see our value within ourselves, and the world will respect us, because we respect ourselves. That will demand respect from men and women

As a travelled entertainer, dancer, singer, model, and teacher, I have dressed in many styles to look good for myself, and the world. My dress styles have been Indian (the sari); the Sulvar Kamiez, which is also Indian; Pakistani; the Japanese Kimono; the Malay Cabaya sarong; the Indonesian Cabaya sarong; and the Chinese cheongsam. The American style, which is many styles and a combination of previous Asian styles, includes my use of scarves to wrap my head while dressing. It was always a plus for me to want to enhance myself as an exotic woman. There were always questions and compliments as to how I did it, and I was asked to demonstrate how it was done. I was always happy to demonstrate. Beauty and its expression are always open to all of us, if we ask.

Performing at Wedding Reception

In dressing, I feel that as women, we can look at different cultural styles and see the beauty, modesty, and pride they show us. We can have our own creative styles and maybe choose some parts of their styles to incorporate with our own. Do your own thing with the many styles that are offered. Our American ingenuity, creativity, and appreciation of the differences of us all includes using those differences for ourselves. My pictures are of my dancing and modeling when I was in my twenties through sixties. I was able to travel the world using those pictures. Now that I'm in my seventies, I look at them and still see the blessing that is given to me to dance, model, photograph, train, and perform with unearned grace.

I'm so thankful for my life, and am truly hopeful that I can impart some of my life experiences to all those who wish to take another look at why life is given to us, as well as our responsibility for seeing, loving, and protecting ourselves for the blessings that life has to offer us.

Many blessings to all those ladies who are aware, and to those ladies who are willing to be aware, in order to learn and be blessed.

Charlotte & Chris,
Dance instructor

Printed in the United States
By Bookmasters